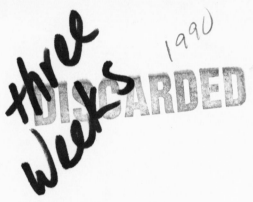

Animal Habitats

The Elephant in the Bush

Text by Ian Redmond

Photographs by the author/ Oxford Scientific Films

Gareth Stevens Publishing
Milwaukee

Contents

Elephants are seldom found far from a source of water. The best elephant habitat is where forest and savanna meet and provide a wide range of food plants.

African Bush Elephants and African Forest Elephants are subspecies of the African Elephant. A Forest Elephant is smaller and has more rounded ears than the African Bush Elephant (above).

Where elephants live

Elephants are the largest land animals on Earth. They are surprisingly adaptable animals and can live in a variety of different *habitats*. In Africa, they are found in cold, misty mountain *rain forests* and also in hot, humid lowland rain forests. They roam across rich grasslands following the rains. But in some areas, they live in near-desert conditions.

Perhaps the best habitat for elephants is actually a mixture, or patchwork, of different habitats. In places where the *savanna* (grassland) is broken up by patches of woodland or where there are winding strips of forest on either side of a river, elephants can make the best use of different sources of food. During the heat of the day, they can *browse* and seek shade under the trees or bathe in the river. Later, they can emerge from the edge of the forest to graze on the open savanna as the Sun sets.

This kind of forest-savanna patchwork once covered most of eastern, central, and southern Africa. Such wild, uncultivated, and unfenced land became known as "the bush" (or, in South Africa, "the bushveldt"). *Bush* comes from the Dutch word *bosch*, meaning a wood or forest. The word soon came to be used for any wilderness area in Africa, whether or not it was wooded. People usually think of the African bush as a vast area of rolling grasslands, dotted with flat-topped Acacia trees and rippling with the backs of innumerable antelope. This picture would seem incomplete without a herd of elephants, ambling along in single file down to a water hole or stretching their trunks high to reach the tastiest tips of the trees. Elephants are an important part of the African landscape in more ways than one.

This extinct Woolly Mammoth lived 10,000 years ago. The fossil bones of its lower jaw were found in South Dakota.

Elephants past and present

A few years before World War I, some soldiers in the British Royal Engineers were digging trenches at the bottom of a chalk cliff at Upnor, beside the Medway River in Kent, England. Suddenly, one of the men noticed that they had just cut through some large bones. The officer in charge stopped them from digging in that spot, but it was another two years before an amateur archaeologist picked up some of the bone fragments and sent them to the British Museum. There, one was identified as a wrist bone of an exceptionally large elephant. In the summer of 1915, an almost complete skeleton was carefully excavated. It became known as the Upnor Elephant and can still be seen today in the Natural History Museum in London, England.

Elephants were common on the banks of the Thames River in England 70,000 years ago, when the Upnor Elephant died, and *fossil* elephant remains have been found in many parts of Europe, Asia, Africa, and North America. But these elephants are not the same as the ones that are alive today. There are now two familiar *species* of elephant in the world: the African Elephant and the Indian (or Asian) Elephant (found in many Asian countries, not just India). But few people realize that about 30 species of true elephant and more than 300 kinds of elephantlike creatures have, in the past, roamed the Earth. The last of these to become extinct was the Woolly Mammoth, which died out only about 10,000 years ago. Deep-frozen mammoth carcasses are sometimes found in the Siberian Arctic. And, astonishingly, the meat — when thawed — is still edible!

Unlikely as it seems, the hyrax (above right) is one of the nearest living relatives of both the African Elephant (bottom) and the Asian Elephant (above left). The elephant's other close relative is the sea cow.

The main feature all these extinct animals had in common with living elephants was the trunk. Other elephantlike features included their large size, rounded feet, and an amazing variety of tusks — ranging from the huge upward-curved tusks of the Imperial Mammoth to the short, downward-pointing, lower-jaw tusks of Deinotherium and the flat, shovel-shaped tusks of Platybelodon. Sadly, out of this wealth of trunk-bearing animals, all but two species are now extinct. Nowadays, even the survival of these last two is in question; their future is in our hands.

Elephants are so different from all other animals that it is difficult to tell which species they are related to. But by comparing the bones of fossil and living elephants with the bones of other *mammals*, zoologists have come to the unlikely conclusion that the closest living relatives of the elephants are hyraxes and sea cows! Recent studies of their body chemistry have confirmed that these three very different types of animal are descended from a common ancestor that lived in North Africa about 55 million years ago.

The Asian Elephant (above left) is more closely related to the extinct mammoth than it is to the African Elephant (below).

The elephant's body

Why are elephants so big? The most obvious benefit comes from the "safety in size" rule: If you are bigger than all the *predators* in your habitat, you are less likely to be killed and eaten. And if, like an elephant, you are a *herbivore*, being taller means that you can reach the foliage other herbivores cannot reach. This is especially advantageous in the dry season, when trees, with their deeper roots, remain green long after the grass has dried and yellowed. Large size also tends to make an animal dominant. The road signs in Africa's national parks say: "Elephants have right of way" — and other animals, as well as motorists, respect the elephant's size.

But there are also disadvantages in being so big. Elephants have evolved many ways to cope with the problems that large size brings. How, for example, do they support and move such a heavy body? An engineer looking at an elephant would see that the backbone is arched like a stone bridge and that the legs, when at rest, are designed like pillars. The bones in each leg are very sturdy and form strong, vertical columns standing on tiptoes. The toenails are very tough, and the flat sole of each foot has ridges

An elephant's foreleg has a round foot, with five toenails; what looks like a knee is actually the wrist. The hind foot is more oval and usually has only four toenails.

An elephant's ears contain blood vessels that lose heat, so by flapping its ears, an elephant keeps cool.

This bull elephant shows three ways of keeping cool. His wrinkled skin holds moisture, he stands in the shade, and he extends his ears to catch a cooling breeze.

of skin, somewhat like a tire tread, to help stop the elephant from slipping. Inside the foot, between the toes, there is a cushion of soft tissue that acts as a shock absorber.

Elephants have powerful neck muscles that they use to lift the weight of their tusks and their massive skull. Inside the skull, the brain does not take up all the space; instead there are many air-filled cavities which help to lessen the weight of the head. In terms of its actual size, an elephant's brain — weighing about 11 lbs (5 kg) — is larger than that of any other land animal, including humans. In proportion to body size, however, the brains of apes are relatively bigger, and the human brain is the biggest of all.

The total weight of a bull African Elephant can be as much as six and a half tons — the same as the combined weight of 80 average-sized men or 400,000 average-sized mice! To produce enough energy to power such a massive body, an elephant has to spend most of its life gathering food — about three-quarters of every day and night is spent feeding. There is also a problem with heat. A large body loses heat much more slowly than a small body because it has proportionately less surface area to lose it from. Every movement of a muscle produces some heat. So elephants would overheat, particularly in open, sunny habitats, if it weren't for their huge ears. The ears have a network of large blood vessels that act like radiator pipes giving off heat. Thus, by flapping their ears to and fro, elephants can cool down on a hot day.

An elephant's nostrils run down the length of its trunk to emerge between the two fingerlike points at the tip.

The trunk

An elephant's trunk is a truly remarkable *organ*. It acts like a fifth limb and has more uses than any other single organ in the animal kingdom. A trunk can do everything your hand and arm can do, everything your nose and lips can do — and a few more things besides! In fact, an elephant uses its trunk to breathe, eat, drink, pick things up, groom, caress, smell, feel, shower (by squirting water), dust-bathe, wrestle, slap, throw, greet, and signal. It can even hold a tool, such as a stick, to scratch an itch it can't quite reach with the end of its trunk alone. So it is hardly surprising to find that *mkono*, the Swahili word for an elephant's trunk, means "hand," not "nose."

The tip of the trunk is used to pull up grass.

Elephants use their trunks to throw dust and mud over themselves, which protects their skin from the Sun and from biting insects and also helps keep them cool.

The trunk is made up of the nose and upper lip, which are joined together and greatly lengthened. Although it acts like a limb, it is unlike any other limb of any *vertebrate* animal because it has no bones in it. Instead of muscles pulling against bones, as in your arm or leg, a trunk moves by means of different sets of muscles contracting against each other. This makes it totally flexible in all directions. Recent research has revealed that there are about 100,000 muscles in an elephant's trunk. Using this array of muscles, the trunk is capable of tremendously powerful actions, such as coiling around and lifting a fallen tree. But it can also perform delicate, precise actions using the tip alone.

While an Asian Elephant's trunk has only one movable projection, or "finger," the tip of the African Elephant's trunk has two. The upper one is like a triangular finger and the lower one is more like a broad, muscular lip. These "fingers" can be used in the same way as we use our forefinger and thumb to pick up small objects. The elephant's nostrils open out between the "fingers" so an elephant can feel something and smell it at the same time. The skin around the trunk tip is very sensitive to touch. Around the nostril openings and over the surface of the trunk, there are short *tactile* hairs to help the elephant feel things.

Elephants also have a very keen sense of smell. At the slightest whiff of danger, an elephant raises its trunk like a nasal periscope to sample the breeze and to find out more about who or what is approaching. In fact, without its trunk, an elephant could not survive. If the trunk is badly injured, for example, in a poacher's snare, an otherwise healthy elephant may waste away and die, unable to drink or feed for itself.

African Forest Elephants have brown tusks that point straight downward, instead of the white, forward-curving tusks of the African Bush Elephant.

Teeth and tusks

Elephants have two kinds of teeth: the front teeth, or incisors, and cheek teeth, or *molars*. There are no incisors in the lower jaw and only two — the tusks — in the upper jaw. The tusks continue to grow throughout an elephant's life, sometimes to enormous lengths. The record length for a tusk is 11.5 ft (3.5 m), and the record weight for a single tusk is 259 lbs (117 kg). Apart from a small conical cap of enamel, which is soon worn away, tusks are made up entirely of ivory, or dentine. Unfortunately for elephants, human beings find ivory very attractive — to the extent that, over the centuries, millions of elephants have been killed for their front teeth. Tusks are solid along most of their length, except for the hollow root which is held in the bones of the face. The root is filled with a fleshy pulp that contains a nerve and blood vessels to feed the growing tooth.

With help from the trunk and a foot, tusks are used to strip bark off trees and to lift heavy objects.

Both male and female African Elephants carry tusks, though the males usually have thicker and longer tusks than females of the same age. Tusks have two main uses: as weapons for fighting and display, and as tools for digging, stripping bark, and levering logs. Some elephants are born without tusks, but fortunately they seem to manage without them. In the Asian species, females seldom have visible tusks. Instead, they usually have little tusks that grow so slowly that they barely protrude out of the mouth. Male Asian Elephants usually do have tusks, although in some regions it is quite common for a proportion of males, known in India as *mucknas*, to be born without any tusks.

The molars are found in both upper and lower jaws toward the back of the elephant's mouth. They grind against each other as the elephant chews its food but do not grow continuously like the tusks. Instead, in each jaw, they grow and wear out one at a time, to be replaced by the next tooth in line. An elephant goes through six sets of teeth during its life, each tooth bigger than the one before. Every tooth is made up of plates, or *lamellae*. These wear down to produce a pattern of ridges on the surface. When the elephant chews, with circular front-to-back movement of the lower jaw, the ridges grind against those on the opposing tooth. When the sixth and final set of teeth wears out (they are enormous — about the size of house bricks), the elephant can no longer eat properly and will soon die. In the wild, this occurs when the animal is about 55 to 65 years old, but some captive Asian Elephants are said to have reached 100 years of age.

Scientists collect elephant jawbones to find out which set of teeth were in use, and therefore how old the animal was, at the time of death.

An elephant uses its trunk to carefully select and prepare each mouthful of food.

By stretching up on two legs, an elephant can reach even higher than a giraffe.

Food and drink

Everything an elephant eats or drinks goes into its body by means of its trunk. When drinking, an elephant sucks nearly 2 gallons (7.6 liters) of water up into its trunk; it then lifts its head to let the water run down its throat. The trunk cannot be used like a drinking straw because, like us, an elephant finds it painful to get water right up its nose. An adult elephant drinks about 50 gallons (189 liters) per day, which is about 25 trunkfuls.

When they feed, elephants may close their eyes or gaze off into the distance. They do not need to look at what they are doing because eating, for an elephant, is largely a matter of touch. Each food plant is carefully selected, plucked, and sometimes prepared before being placed in the mouth by the trunk tip. To a human observer, it can almost seem as though the trunk has a will of its own, as it feels around in a thicket, stuffing one morsel after another into the elephant's mouth.

The size of each food item may vary greatly, since elephants eat different parts of a wide range of different plants. With the delicate "fingers" at the tip of their trunk, they can pick off individual leaves, seed pods, or fruits. This technique is especially useful when dealing with spiny plants, such as Acacia trees. An elephant may curl the end of its trunk around a stem and

Elephants drink only once or twice a day as a rule. They don't seem to mind whether the water is clear or muddy, as long as there is plenty of it.

strip off all the leaves along its length; or it might break off the whole branch and then chew off the leafy twigs from the end. The elephant may eat the branch itself, provided it is small enough for the molars to crush easily — about 1 inch (2.5 cm) in diameter. Larger branches may be chewed to remove the bark, which the elephant then eats.

Elephants strip bark from mature trees by chiseling behind it with their tusks. They then haul the bark away from the tree trunk with their own trunk. This activity often kills the trees. With one tree in particular, the Baobab or "upside-down tree," elephants actually like to eat the pulpy wood. So they often carve out great holes in the side of the smooth, gray, bottle-shaped tree trunks.

Elephants eat an enormous amount — something like 330 to 500 lbs (150-225 kg) per day, depending on the size of the elephant and the kind of vegetation. At first glance, life for an elephant appears to be a nonstop feast. In fact, they have three main feeding periods — one in the morning, one in the afternoon, and one around midnight. And feeding may be interrupted at any time by social activities or the need to rest or to travel.

Trees in the bush show a level "browse line," which shows the height to which elephants can reach.

Elephants visit salt licks, but because their tongues are not long enough, they cannot lick. Instead, they use their tusks like a pitchfork to loosen the soil before they eat.

The elephant's appetite for salt

All animals need salt in their diet. This is why food tastes better with salt. Our bodies simply could not work without it. But too much salt can also be a problem. People seem to have lost the ability to know when they have had enough salt. But, animals instinctively know how to regulate how much salt they eat. When an animal needs salt, it will seek out a supply. When it has had enough, though, it stops eating it. The salt it eats may not always be common salt (sodium chloride) — other mineral salts will often do instead.

A herd of cows and calves stretch their trunks to search for salty bits of soil at a salt lick; they sometimes suck up salty dust and blow it into their mouths.

An elephant family slowly files into the depths of Kitum Cave to mine salty rock. Cows keep a motherly trunk on their calves to keep them safe in the total darkness.

The hunger for salt, or "salt appetite," occurs when there is a shortage of salt in any region. In the rain forests of East Africa, for example, the rain dissolves the soluble salts out of the soil. As a result, the plants that grow in these soils do not contain much salt, and any herbivore that feeds on these plants will have a salt-deficient diet. When elephants are hungry for salt, they tend to dig at any exposed soil or rock with their tusks and taste it. If it turns out to be salty, they start eating it, and the place soon becomes known to the local animals as a valuable salt lick.

Elephants dig the soil or rock and then sweep up the bits with their trunk and lift them into their mouth. There, the massive molars grind up the larger particles and the whole lot is swallowed. An elephant may eat about 55 lbs (25 kg) of soil during an hour-long visit to a salt lick; if the salt lick is in a cliff, the elephants will gradually dig out an overhang.

In some places, this digging into cliffs has produced small caves, but usually the roof will collapse before the cave becomes very big. There is only one place in the world where elephant digging has apparently produced deep caves, and that is on Mount Elgon, an extinct volcano on the border between Kenya and Uganda. One such cave, known as Kitum, extends 525 feet (160 m) horizontally into the mountain; it is about 13 feet (4 m) high and 130 feet (40 m) wide at the entrance, increasing to a width of 330 feet (100 m) inside. The idea that such a huge cavern could have been dug by elephants does seem incredible. But scientists studying the cave — and the animals that use it — think it may have been formed by elephant mining activity over many thousands of years. Each new generation of elephants has learned from its parents how to mine the salty rock deep underground. And year after year, the cave continues to grow as the elephants carry away quantities of rock in their stomachs.

Bull elephants will sniff at females, or at patches of their dung and urine, to see if they are in heat.

Courtship and birth

Adult male and female elephants normally live apart. So when a female is in heat — that is, ready to mate — her body gives off a special scent to alert any nearby males. When a bull elephant meets a herd of cows, he will sniff around them, then curl the tip of his trunk up into his mouth. There, the scent of a female in heat is detected by the Jacobson's organ, two small openings in the roof of the mouth.

If one of the cows is ready to mate, courtship may begin. The bull will follow her around, sometimes for hours, sniffing and touching her with his trunk. At the same time, he will be doing his best to chase away any smaller bulls (and hoping, no doubt, that no larger bulls show up to chase him away). Eventually he will approach her, intending to mate.

Courtship also involves gentle caressing with the trunk; mating usually takes place away from the rest of the herd.

Elephant calves always stay close to their mothers — this one is just two weeks old.

After caressing each other with their trunks, the female usually runs away. If she stops, the bull approaches her from behind and lays his trunk and tusks along her back. Mating then takes less than a minute, but the pair will probably mate many times over the next few days.

When a cow is first in heat, she will probably be chased by, and may even mate with, several bulls. After a day or two, however, the males become more aggressive toward one another. Eventually, the most powerful bull elephant will have dominated all the others, and only he will breed with that cow. This means that the *sperm* from the strongest bull is most likely to *fertilize* the female's egg, thereby increasing the chance of a strong and healthy offspring.

The elephant's *gestation* period is the longest in the animal kingdom — about 22 months. During this time, a single baby (very occasionally twins) grows inside its mother's womb. By the time it is born, the calf will weigh about 200 lbs (90 kg). When a female feels the first signs of giving birth, she may move away from the rest of the herd. Another female, usually a more experienced relative, often accompanies her. With this "midwife" in attendance, the pregnant female then pushes hard to force the new calf out. Within half an hour of being born, the calf will normally have staggered to its feet on wobbly legs and taken its first faltering steps. Its mother and the other females are always ready to offer a helping trunk if necessary. From that moment on, the baby elephant will stick close by its mother night and day.

To suckle, a calf flips its nose over its head and uses its mouth; the mother stands with her foreleg forward so her calf can find the nipple.

Family life

Baby elephants are born into a matriarchal society. This means that the females are in charge. An old female, the matriarch, leads the herd, which is made up of her sisters, daughters, granddaughters, and their offspring. When spread out to feed, large herds often break up into smaller groups. Each smaller group is usually a family unit that consists of one or two mothers and their calves. The herd as a whole is called a "kinship group" because all the families are usually related.

As with humans, the young elephant's first and strongest ties are with its mother. As it gets older, however, it gradually meets more and more members of the herd — especially the playful older calves. If the play gets rough or if there is danger — either real or imagined — a calf will instantly take shelter between its mother's front legs.

Although a baby elephant can walk very soon after birth, not all of its muscles are well coordinated. In particular, a calf has no idea how to control the rubbery combination hose and pipe that flops around in front of its face! It takes a year or more to master those hundred thousand muscles in the trunk. So until then, the baby elephant drinks like any other baby, with its mouth. The cow elephant has a pair of breasts between her front legs.

Each calf follows its mother as they move off after bathing. The water-mark shows that the mothers waded up to their belly, while the small calf was almost submerged.

Her nipples point sideways and are upturned, making it easy for the calf to reach one when it stands beside her. Baby elephants suckle on the basis of "little and often." They are dependent on their mother's milk for about two years. But older calves will sometimes try to suckle, too, perhaps when they need some maternal comfort. At about two and a half years of age, the calf's tusks begin to show. Breast-feeding a young tusker must be uncomfortable, so the cows usually discourage suckling after this age. Some mothers, however, have been seen nursing calves of up to nine years of age.

Elephants reach sexual maturity at about 10 to 12 years of age. Immature females, and females without new calves, will often act as "aunties" by baby-sitting and generally keeping an eye on the youngsters in the herd. This sharing of duties sometimes goes as far as one mother's allowing another female's young calf to suckle her. There are even reported cases in which a female has adopted a calf whose mother had been killed.

A cow elephant usually has calves every four or five years, so the first calf can feed itself before the second one arrives. But an elder calf still spends a lot of time near its mother for comfort and reassurance.

When sparring, young bulls push and charge at each other, clash their tusks together, and wrestle with their trunks, but this play fighting rarely leads to bloodshed.

Bachelor life

When a bull elephant reaches puberty, he will soon have to leave the family herd. If, by the time he is about 15 years old, he is still spending too much time with the herd, the adult cows will keep chasing him off. Eventually, he will be forced to leave and join a bachelor herd. Female elephants, as they grow older, play less and less often. The play of young males, however, develops into a sort of mock combat. This friendly sparring allows them to test their strength and to sort out their position in the male social order. The weaker bull elephants soon come to recognize the stronger ones and give way accordingly.

But every so often, bull elephants go wild. Asian Elephant bulls have long been known to go through a regular period of unpredictable, aggressive behavior known as musth. During this time, a sticky fluid oozes from the bull's *temporal gland* between the eye and the ear. Until recently, it was thought that musth only occurred in Asian bulls, but it has now been confirmed in African Elephants, too. In the African species, both sexes often have a fluid trickling from their temporal glands, but this alone is not a sign of musth. It is only when the male's fluid becomes dark and sticky, and when the elephant becomes more aggressive and sexually active, that an African bull is said to be in musth. In some ways, this behavior is similar to the rutting of male deer; the difference is that stags rut only during the mating season, while elephants have no particular season for either musth or mating.

A bull elephant chases a smaller bull away. Elephants can walk at up to 15 miles per hour (24 kph); this is not a run because one foot is always on the ground.

Musth is best explained as a short period of risk taking. While in this state, a bull will rush around with his head carried high, challenging every male he comes across — including larger and more dominant bulls. Young males, for whom a serious fight with a big bull might prove fatal, have only a short musth. As they get older, their musth period lasts longer each year. By the time they have reached their prime, between 30 and 50 years of age, their musth will last for two or three months. The rest of the year is spent quietly feeding to build up their strength.

Spectacular battles take place between bulls in musth, but the reward is worth the risk of serious injury or even death. The winner can claim a high status and the chance to mate with any cows in heat at the time.

Bull elephants only stay near the family herd if a cow is in heat. But if the elephants have been attacked by poachers, the bulls will help defend the herd.

Smell is the elephant's most important sense. When they greet one another, elephants usually sample each other's breath.

Communication

Elephants use several of their senses to communicate with each other, but as with humans, sound is the most important means. They do not have a true language, but elephants can certainly show their feelings; they rumble, roar, trumpet, squeal, gurgle, and chirp to one another. But there is more to these calls than first meets the ear. Recent research has revealed that two-thirds of what an elephant says is inaudible to humans. By playing back tape recordings at ten times normal speed, scientists have discovered that elephants also call to one another using infrasounds — low-frequency sounds that are below the level of human hearing.

In the bush, infrasonic elephant rumbles can carry for miles. This explains how elephants are able to arrive together at the same place from several different directions — something that has long puzzled human observers. When the elephants do meet, they exchange a special "greeting rumble." If they are separated, one may give a "where are you?" call and then stand listening, with ears spread, to hear the "I'm over here!" rumble in reply. There is also the "let's go" rumble, when one member of a group decides it is time to move on, and there are sexual rumbles, made only by males in musth and females in heat.

An elephant spreads its ears wide like this to send a mild threat signal to another animal — in this case, to the photographer!

Elephants send visual signals by moving their ears and trunk. If an elephant feels threatened by something, it will make itself look even bigger than it really is by putting on a special display called "standing tall." In this display, the elephant stretches itself up to its full height, spreads its ears, and looks down its nose at whatever it is afraid of. An elephant that feels more confident, and wants to frighten another animal, uses a different display. It may trumpet and shake its head — which makes the ears crack like whips against the side of its body. Then it might take a couple of paces forward and stand tall with ears wide. Finally, the elephant may make an impressive mock charge, but this is a bluff that is of little danger to the observer. If, on the other hand, the elephant curls its trunk up, keeps its ears flat, and runs straight at the source of danger, it is making a real attack that it will carry through regardless of the source of danger.

Elephants also use chemical communication. The smell of a female in heat, for example, alerts any passing males. A cow elephant also recognizes her own calf by its unique smell. And a male in musth will rub the sticky fluid from his temporal glands onto twigs and branches. This acts as a smelly signpost, telling other elephants that he is in musth and has recently passed that way.

Lastly, elephants also touch each other to communicate, especially if they are upset. Like humans and apes, a gentle touch or caress will calm and reassure a tense or frightened individual.

Old elephants may doze on their feet, but most elephants sleep lying down — for four hours after midnight and, as shown here, for an hour or so during the heat of the day.

Some birds like to follow elephants around; these egrets will fly over the river to meet the elephants on the other side. They snap up insects that are disturbed by the elephants' feet as they walk through the grass.

Elephants and other bush animals

Being the largest living land animal means that almost all other animals give way to elephants. There are few exceptions to this rule. Sometimes an angry rhinoceros might succeed in chasing off an elephant, and on one occasion, a silverback, or dominant male, Mountain Gorilla was seen beating its chest at a group of four forest elephants, whereupon they repeatedly backed down from his advances. But the fact is that in an out-and-out contest, elephants can literally walk all over any other animal.

It is obvious, however, that elephants hardly ever do this. Their size means that most other animals actively avoid them, so confrontations are rare. Young elephants, however, will stick their ears out and charge at anything from a bird to a butterfly, apparently just for fun. If a pride of lions or pack of hyenas or hunting dogs is near a herd, the matriarch will probably chase them away. Baby elephants occasionally fall prey to large carnivores that hunt in groups. Calves have also been killed by large Nile Crocodiles. But apart from such rare cases, only very weak or dying elephants are likely to end up as the victims of a predator.

There have been some strange sightings of elephants chasing lions or cheetahs from their kills and then standing guard over the remains of the prey, but no one has been able to explain why they do this. It may be associated with their equally mysterious interest in dead bodies and bones.

Elephants generally live peacefully alongside other herbivores. This Impala ram grazes without taking any notice of the nearby elephant.

Elephants do not go to a special "graveyard" to die, but they do pick up and scatter the bones of long-dead elephants. There are also reports of them covering up dead elephants with branches and soil.

Some animals in the bush benefit directly from elephants. In forest habitats, elephants keep trails open through the densest bamboo thickets and undergrowth. Trees felled by elephants provide ground-level food for smaller browsing herbivores. And in dry areas, water holes and mud wallows dug by elephants can be lifesavers for other forms of wildlife in times of drought.

A charging elephant is a fearful sight and will drive away a pride of lions or any other predator — except a human with a gun.

Traditionally, elephants have the right of way in African national parks, but in places where poaching is out of control, elephants are now afraid of vehicles.

Elephants and people

People have always loved elephants, but this has never stopped us from exploiting them in many ways. For centuries, people have killed elephants for their ivory and captured their young for training. We have made elephants fight in wars and have harnessed their strength to work long hours. We dress them up and make them stand on one leg in the circus ring, and we lock them up, often alone, in zoos. And yet — ask anyone — people say they love elephants.

Asian Elephants have been trained in countries such as India, Myanmar (Burma), and Thailand for thousands of years. They carried kings and maharajahs, pulled huge carts, and hauled timber from the forest. Even with today's modern machinery, there are still some places where only an elephant can go to haul out a teak or mahogany log.

This orphan, whose mother was shot by poachers, may one day return to the wild. The tent makes the calf feel more secure, like a mother's flank to suckle against.

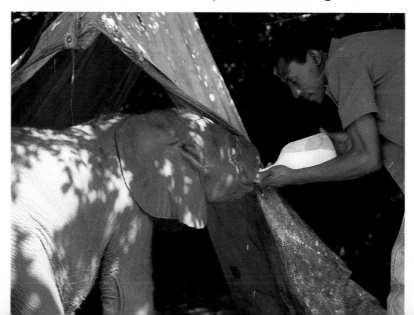

People used to hunt tigers from elephants' backs. Nowadays, trained Asian Elephants carry parties of tourists who shoot the tigers with cameras instead of guns.

Elephants still play an important role in cultural and religious festivals in many Asian countries. But there are no similar traditions in Africa. This has led many people to believe that African Elephants are untrainable. In fact, historically, African Elephants have been trained to work for at least as long as the Asian species. Aristotle, the Greek philosopher and writer, described their use in the fourth century BC. In 218 BC, Hannibal, the Carthaginian general, took 37 war elephants through Spain and over the Alps to help his army attack the Romans in Italy. It won him a place in the history books, but only one elephant survived to take part in the victory parade. Once the Roman army learned to defeat war elephants, their use declined. African Elephants have seldom been trained for work since then.

In Western countries, our only chance of seeing an elephant today, other than saving up to go on a safari, is to visit a circus or zoo. But do we see the complete animal if it is in a leafless yard or stall? What makes an elephant what it is comes to more than just the animal itself — it is the animal interacting with its natural *environment*. Nevertheless, some captive elephants are now being given a better life; a few forward-thinking zoos now keep small herds in large, open paddocks. Furthermore, the better zoos are now working together to share the few breeding bulls in captivity. If elephant numbers continue to decline in the wild, the small population of captive animals may one day be vital to the survival of both species.

Millions of elephants have died to supply the demand for ivory carvings, such as these in a Hong Kong ivory "factory." A recent report estimated that 80 percent of the world ivory trade is from illegally killed elephants.

The use and abuse of ivory

Ivory is a beautiful substance, both to look at and to touch. Because of its beauty, people have been carving ivory for almost as long as they have been carving anything. Some of the earliest known works of art, the Aurignacian Venuses, are made of ivory. These round female forms — possibly fertility symbols — were carved in mammoth ivory 27,000 years ago. Today, there are rich traditions of ivory carving in many countries. Unfortunately, this means that the demand for ivory has long been greater than the supply from legal hunting or from animals that die naturally. Elephants are therefore killed illegally because poachers and unscrupulous business people have an endless market for ivory. Sadly, it is obvious that the supply of elephants is NOT endless.

Clearly, the ivory artisans and legal traders do not want elephants to become extinct — otherwise they would go out of business. It is the illegal ivory trade that threatens elephant populations in most of Africa. The loss of habitat for farmland is also a threat, but some of the worst declines in elephant numbers have taken place in supposedly protected national parks where farming is banned. If conservationists cannot successfully protect the elephants and their habitat, the species may become extinct in the wild. If that were to happen, the artistic skills of generations of ivory carvers would also disappear.

This tusk was carved in Africa, then sold to a tourist who tried to bring it to Britain without an import permit. It was confis-cated by the customs service.

Rangers weigh and measure tusks from elephants of all ages — even calves — killed by poachers on Mount Elgon, Kenya.

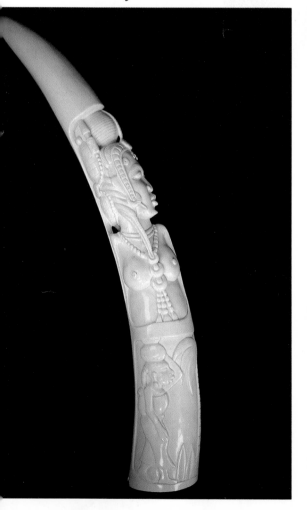

Life in the bush

When you see the devastation left behind by a herd of feeding elephants, it would be easy to think of them as destructive and wasteful eaters. Trees are pushed over, branches and bark may be torn off standing trees, while smaller plants are uprooted and squashed underfoot. In addition, much of what the elephants eat seems to pass through their bodies with very little being digested. But despite this apparent destruction, elephants play a vital role in their environment — as shown in the diagram below.

When they push over trees in forest habitats, elephants open up the *canopy* and let in more light. This allows more plants to grow beneath the trees, which means more food for ground-dwelling animals. Elephants eat a wide variety of different plants, many of which depend on the elephants to help spread their seeds. When elephants eat fruit, for example, many of the seeds will pass through the gut undamaged. The seeds soon grow in the dung, which is a good fertilizer, perhaps miles from the parent plant. When elephants move from browsing in the forest to grazing on the grassland, they continue to drop seeds in their dung. This enables forest plants to spread onto the savanna, thereby encouraging the forest-savanna patchwork that is the elephants' ideal habitat.

The ecological relationships of the African Elephant

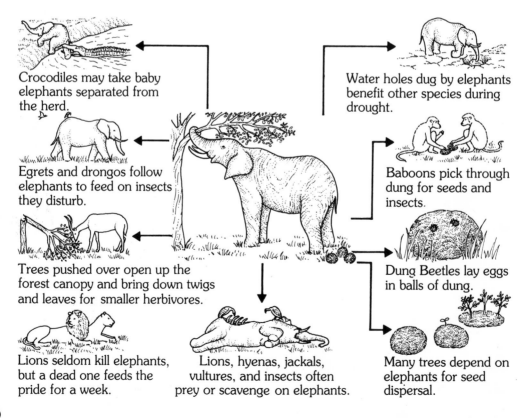

Crocodiles may take baby elephants separated from the herd.

Water holes dug by elephants benefit other species during drought.

Egrets and drongos follow elephants to feed on insects they disturb.

Baboons pick through dung for seeds and insects.

Trees pushed over open up the forest canopy and bring down twigs and leaves for smaller herbivores.

Dung Beetles lay eggs in balls of dung.

Lions seldom kill elephants, but a dead one feeds the pride for a week.

Lions, hyenas, jackals, vultures, and insects often prey or scavenge on elephants.

Many trees depend on elephants for seed dispersal.

The African Elephant has been roaming the bush for three million years. It is up to us to make sure that the species survives beyond the next few decades.

Sadly, however, the Africa of today is not the same as the Africa in which elephants evolved. Where elephants do survive, they are hemmed in by humanity. As more and more land is covered by fences and fields, roads and cities, we humans are squeezing out the elephants in both Africa and Asia. The only hope for their long-term survival is in the national parks and reserves, but these are like islands of elephants in a sea of people. In places where protection of the wildlife is poor, the ivory poachers are wiping out whole populations of elephants. Where wildlife protection is good, the number of elephants may increase so fast that the land cannot support them. The elephants then destroy the trees faster than new trees can grow to replace them. If the elephants try to migrate out of the park, they are shot for raiding crops. If they stay, the park warden has to decide whether to kill some of the elephants, or whether to let them die slowly of starvation, until their numbers fall to a level that allows the vegetation to recover.

In their natural state, elephants do not destroy their habitat; instead, they are a vital part of it. The challenge facing people today is how to preserve enough elephant habitat for that natural balance to return and how to protect the elephants from ivory poachers. Only then will the world's largest and most majestic land animal have a future in the wild.

Glossary and Index

These new words about elephants appear in the text on the pages shown after each definition. Each new word first appears in the text in *italics*, just as it appears here.

browse ....to eat leaves and buds of trees, as eaten by a browsing herbivore (as opposed to a grazing herbivore, which eats grass). **3, 13**

canopy ....the layer of leaves at the top of trees. **30**

environment . an animal's (or person's) surroundings. **27, 30**

fertilize ....to make fertile, especially when a male sperm cell enters a female's egg to begin the development of a baby. **17**

fossil ....the mineralized remains of an ancient animal or plant found in rock. **4, 5**

gestation ......the period of development of a baby mammal from the fertilization of an egg to the birth. **17**

habitat ....the natural home of any plant or animal. **2, 3, 6, 7, 29-31**

herbivore ......an animal that eats plants. **6, 15, 25, 30**

lamellae ....the flattened plates of dentine and enamel, each with its own root, which attach to each other to make up an elephant's molars. **11**

mammals .....animals with hair or fur that feed their young on milk. **5**

molars ....the cheek teeth (grinding teeth) of elephants. **10, 11, 13, 15**

organ ....a group of tissues in the body that combine to perform a particular function. **8, 16**

predator ....an animal that kills and eats other animals. **6, 24, 25**

rain forest ....a forest that depends upon a high rainfall to grow. **3, 15**

savanna ....flat, open grassland with occasional trees. **2, 3, 30**

species ....a particular kind of animal or plant that is capable of breeding with its own kind. **4-5, 11, 20, 27, 29-31**

sperm ....the tadpole-shaped male reproductive cell. **17**

tactile ....concerning, or having, the sense of touch. **9**

temporal gland............a small gland with an opening between an elephant's eye and ear. It secretes a dark, oily liquid called temporin that may act as a chemical signal between elephants. **20, 23**

vertebrate .....an animal with a backbone. Vertebrates include fish, amphibians, reptiles, birds, and mammals. **9**

Reading level analysis: FRY 5.5, FLESCH 83 (easy), RAYGOR 6.5, SPACHE 4, FOG 4.5, SMOG 3.5

Library of Congress Cataloging-in-Publication Data

Redmond, Ian.
The elephant in the bush.

(Animal habitats)
Summary: Text and photographs depict elephants feeding, breeding, and defending themselves in their natural habitats.
1. Elephants--Juvenile literature. [1. Elephants] I. Oxford Scientific Films. II. Title. III. Series.
QL737.P98R44 1989   599.6'1   89-11297
ISBN 0-8368-0116-4

North American edition first published in 1990 by Gareth Stevens Children's Books, RiverCenter Building, Suite 201, 1555 North RiverCenter Drive, Milwaukee, WI 53212, USA. Text copyright © 1990 by Oxford Scientific Films. All rights reserved. No part of this book may be reproduced in any form or by any means without permission in writing from Gareth Stevens, Inc.

Conceived, designed, and produced by Belitha Press Ltd., London. Consultant Editor: Jennifer Coldrey. Art Director: Treld Bicknell. Design: Naomi Games. US Editors: Mark J. Sachner and Valerie Weber. Line Drawings: Lorna Turpin.

The author and publishers wish to thank the following for permission to reproduce copyright material: Ian Redmond for title page and pp. 5 above right, 6 left, 7, 8 above, 9, 10 above, 13 below, 14 both, 15, 16 above, 21 both, 22 both, 24, 25 above, 26 both, 28, and 29 both; **Oxford Scientific Films** for p. 2 (Edwin Sadd); p. 3 (G. I. Bernard); p. 4 (Charles Palek); pp. 5 above left and 27 (M. J. Coe); pp. 5 below, 17, and 18 (Maurice Tibbles); p. 6 right (Sean Morris); pp. 8 below, 12 left, 20, and front cover (Anthony Bannister); pp. 10 above, 16 below, 19 above, and 25 below (David Cayless); p. 11 (Robert Buxton); p. 12 right (Gerald Thompson); p. 13 above (John Paling); p. 19 below (Stan Osolinski); p. 23 and back cover (Richard Packwood); p. 31 (Michael Fogden).

Printed in the United States of America
1 2 3 4 5 6 7 8 9 96 95 94 93 92 91 90

For a free color catalog describing Gareth Stevens' list of high-quality children's books, call 1-800-341-3569.